9 Ways To Boost Confidence As A Model

By Xavier Gelsey
Illustrated by Remus
Stanley IV

Why I Wrote This Book?

I wrote this book as a guide for women who are interested in modeling and need advice on boosting their confidence. Even if you are already modeling, this book can help models increase their confidence even more. This book will help them know different ways to be more secured in themselves as models. Even if you may not want to model, confidence is a foundation as a woman in whatever

you do. If a woman does not have

confidence in herself, neither will

anyone else.

Table of Contents

Chapter 1
Faith with Feeling

So now you want to be a model. You may have had aspirations of being a model that came about when you were a child, sometime in your teenage life, or even your adult life. No matter what motivated you to be a model, a lot of women need a confidence booster to help them on their journey of modeling.

Do you have what it takes mentally? What do you believe about yourself? Do you believe that you can be a model? Do you see yourself walking down an NYC Fashion Week runway? Do you believe in yourself to be the next great Naomi Campbell, Gisele Bundchen or Cindy Crawford? Or Do you believe that you can be that next print model for a catalog or your local boutique?

All these questions resonate with the aspect of faith. Do you believe in your mind, heart, and soul that you are a great model? If you don't highly believe in yourself as a model, nobody else will either. This is imperative when you work with fashion designers for the runway. This is also important if you are auditioning for model castings. If you can see yourself as a great model, then you can manifest yourself to be that great model.

As a model, it wasn't enough for people to tell me that I was beautiful for me to become a model. I had to see myself as such and believe that for myself. Although I had to get through some challenges, I had to constantly remind myself that "I am a great supermodel," even though our society tried to give women an outer appearance of what a model should look like. I am happy that the barriers of how a model should look are being broken.

No matter what, build your faith by telling yourself that you can do anything you put your mind to, and have a higher belief in yourself and in God, The Universe, or

Supreme Being. The best way to tell yourself this is to look at yourself in the mirror and practice posing as a model. Passionately speak out loud about your faith in yourself. Now you may not feel anything at first, but as your subconscious mind starts to yield to your words, the feeling will follow.

Secondly, visualize yourself being a model. Meditate for at least 5 minutes on being that top print or runway model and smile while you're doing it to provoke that happy feeling on being a successful and prosperous model. Do these daily to make your faith strong as a model.

You will also build your faith as a model by wearing fashionable clothes that can provoke that feeling. Faith is the main part of your wardrobe for your confidence and your confidence is the necessary wardrobe for your modeling!

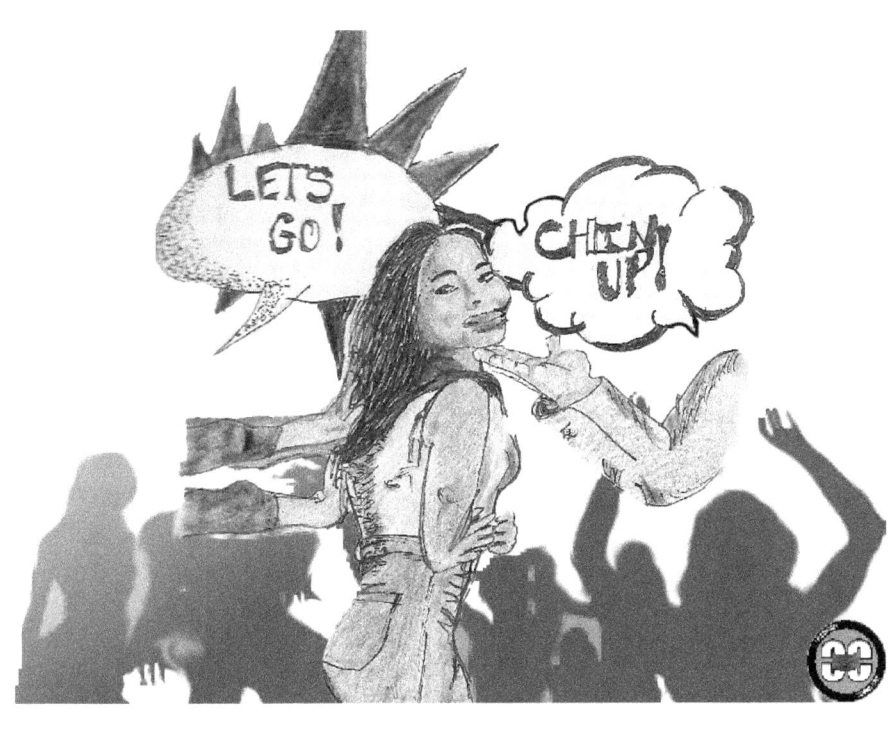

Chapter 2
No Hope Deferred

Along the way you can get discouraged about being a model which can put a damper on your confidence. Whether it is someone saying something negative to you or you not getting chosen as the model for a casting call or opportunity. Sometimes distractions and situations can cause you to lose hope as a model.

The number one tip that I can offer is to stay persistent and consistent in your modeling. Do not stop posing in the mirror, or saying your confidence affirmations, which I will talk about a little later. Don't stop doing photo shoots or taking photos of yourself to put online to build your portfolio.

Do not give up on yourself! My persistency and consistency in my model routine has boosted my confidence, which has led to great opportunities for me such as working and promoting for a local boutique here in Jacksonville, Florida. Looking at YouTube videos of models that look like you will also encourage you on your modeling journey. One of my favorite models I love watching on YouTube is Tyra Banks.

I love Tyra Banks because she went through some challenges in the model business. One of the challenges she had to face was not being as slim as the other models in the business and people in the industry always reminded her of that. She did slim down, but her curves did not go anywhere. I remember her saying she grew up being a chubby little girl and that she has always had curves. She embraced them and became a symbol for many women of color who also have curves. She inspired them to embrace their curves as well. This helped me to continue to stride and slay my race in my own lane as a model.

Another thing I love about Tyra Banks is how she rips the runway. She brings so much life and she really changed the traditional runway concept for Victoria Secret. This taught me about being adaptive without conforming to the industry. All these things ignited my hope as a model.

Chapter 3
Self-Love

Love is the greatest gift of all. It helps to fuse the other two modeling foundational keys (faith and hope) together. You have to have love for yourself in order to really succeed. Your love is a guiding light to your confidence.

I know that there are temptations in society that can provoke you to not love yourself, whether it is the color of your skin or not having the stereotypical supermodel body of a size 4. It could be not being as curvy or having the biggest size breasts and booty like those vixens in the Playboy magazines and music videos. There can be a variety of sources that can influence women to hate themselves and provoke them to seek permanent change to their bodies.

By no means am I saying that we should not enhance ourselves, add to our natural beauty or change our look for self-improvement. No matter the means of change, make sure it is for the right reasons and not out of insecurity. Make sure all these changes are done out of love. As much as I love my makeup, wigs, weaves, and my versatile looks as a model; as a woman, I embrace my natural look and hair.

As a woman going into modeling, it is important that you love yourself with your flaws and all. Even if you have physical goals as a model, love yourself through your self-improvement and changes. Get comfortable at looking at yourself in the mirror and smiling at yourself. If you can be comfortable looking at yourself in front of the mirror, then you will be more comfortable posing in front of a camera.

Chapter 4
Positive Affirmations

You have to take the right actions to build faith, hope, and love for yourself. One of the major ways to do that is to speak to yourself with love so that your confidence is continuously progressing. What are you saying when you see yourself in the mirror? Confidence affirmations are important for your walk in the limelight as a model.

Here are some affirmations you can say to yourself that will help you with your confidence as a model:

1.   I am a top paid supermodel.

2.   I can do anything I put my mind to.

3.   I love myself.

        I am true to myself.

        I love my body.

I accept myself for who I am.

I can do all things through Christ who strengthen me (Phil. 4:19).

I am a successful fashion print model.

4. I am a successful runway model.

5. I am at my desired weight as a model.

6. I believe in myself.

7. I am a healthy model.

8. I am only thinking the right thoughts about myself.

9. I am confident as a model.

10. I am becoming more and more confident in my ability as a model.

11. Each day and every way, I am improving more and more as a model.

12. I have the right look as a model.

13. I am beautiful.

14. I am a prosperous model.

15.   I walk with confidence as a model.

        You can add and modify these affirmations to make them applicable to you. I would also highly recommend you to listen to Justin Perry's audio on YouTube under "You Are Creators" called "Confidence Affirmations." I highly recommend you say these affirmations for at least 21 to 30 days to make it a habit. Take a step further and say them for 3 months to make it a lifestyle.

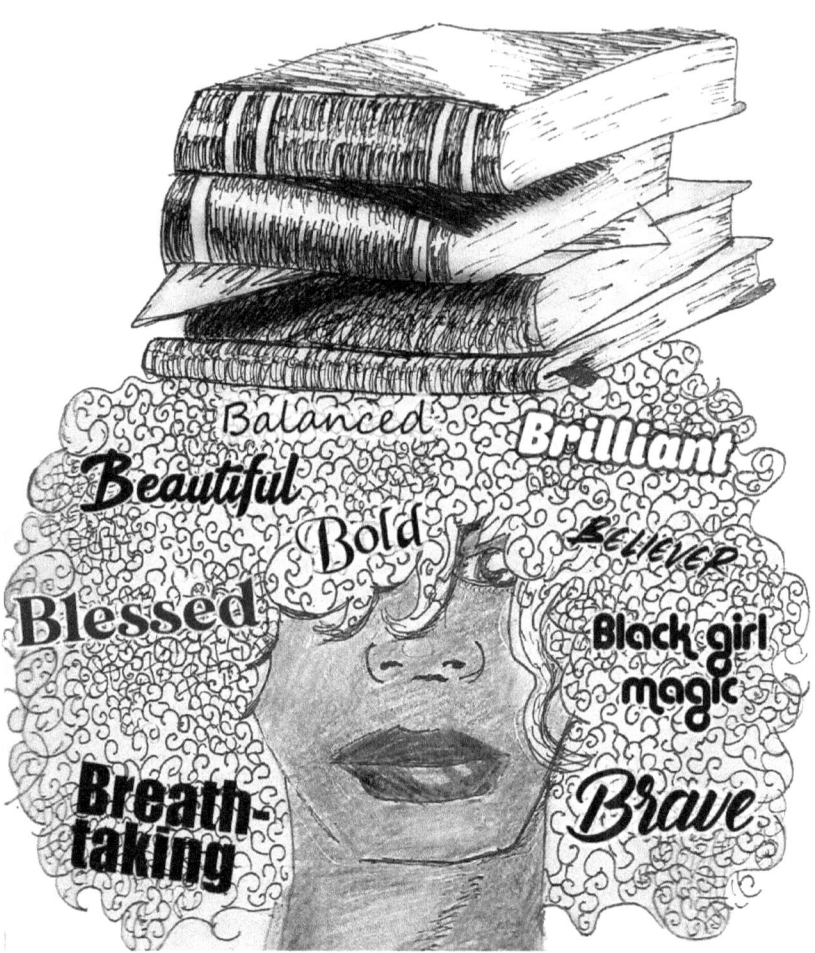

13

Chapter 5
Model Coach/Mentor

Another stepping stone to building yourself up as a model is having a mentor. You also need to make sure you have the right model coach. This person should believe in you as a model wholeheartedly and will push you to manifest your greatest output as a model. This should be someone that will boost, and give your confidence an upward jolt.

Now keep in mind that they will critique you but, they are doing that to make you a better model, not a bitter model. The first model trainer I had told me that I should stop doing a pose that I was initially doing during practice. I didn't take it personal, I took it as a tip that would help me grow as a model. I started learning and doing better poses.

My second one whom played a major role in my life showed me how to walk, gave me tips on how to model, and gave me a lot of other sound advice. Both mentors gave me the advice on practicing my walk and poses that I still do today. The advice and training that I got from my coaches and mentors helped me to stop being timid when walking in front of a lot of people on a runway and when posing in front of them. Their advice and training also helped me to become comfortable in front of the camera.

My modeling coaches and mentors helped to get in the mindset of being a model, for example, Rodney explained to me that even if someone says something to me that is personal, don't take it personal. I still use his advice today with my modeling as well as in other areas of my life. His advice helped me to not let people's words hurt my ego.

Danielle told me to walk up in any casting call saying to myself, "I'm the baddest chick on earth." She told me to walk like a queen and make my presence known. She also told me to walk like I own that casting call and that I already have it. She was indirectly telling me to work my faith.

Chapter 6
Practice Is Golden

I know the saying "Practice makes perfect" is a cliché to many people, and there is some truth in that cliché. However, I will further say practice doesn't make you perfect, it makes you better. If it made you perfect, you wouldn't need to practice anymore. Practice makes you prepared for whatever it is you are prepping yourself to do.

In modeling, practice is imperative when you are attending a casting call, getting ready to rip that runway or if you have a major photoshoot coming up. It can release all those nerves and insecurities you may be feeling prior to the project or event. I'm not saying you won't get nervous when you perform, but practice can help you deal with your nerves so that you're able to better control them.

When you practice your modeling, it can boost your self-esteem. The more you practice, the less you will feel intimidated by your fellow models and your audience. When I started modeling, I was a little intimidated by models who had more experience than me when it came to walking the runway. As I began to practice my walk daily and adding my style to it, those insecure thoughts began to diminish.

It became easier for me to walk on a stage in front of a lot of people. I was practicing my walk for 5 minutes daily. It was worth the investment for my self-esteem as a model. I was practicing my walk and even my poses as though I was already there on stage or doing a major photoshoot.

Another reason that I was practicing my poses was to get comfortable in front of the camera. As my photoshoots progressed, I was more relaxed and less tense for the photographer. It was easy for the photographer to work with me. I would suggest to you to practice your poses in front of a mirror. It helps you to be more at ease when you can see yourself as you're practicing your poses. It allows you to get a better look at what they look like. If you can be comfortable with yourself in front of a mirror, then you can be comfortable in front of a camera and anybody you must perform for.

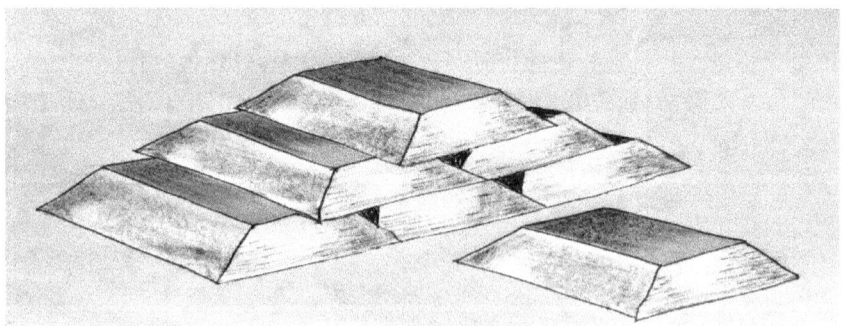

Chapter 7
Self-Care

Self-care is the outer works of your self-love. They go hand in hand. Taking care of yourself will give you the energy of self-confidence. It gives you a winning edge as a model.

One of the thing you need to do as a model for your self-care is to use discipline and self-control when it comes to what you eat. I am not going to tell you which diet you need to get on because I am going to leave that to your discretion and because I am not a physician. Learn as a model to use moderation in what you drink and eat. Food does affect your mood, and you want to have the right mood whenever you're at a casting call or doing a photoshoot. This will help you to bring a better, more confident you.

Make sure as a model you are keeping yourself physically active. Whether it is cardio, yoga, taking the stairs, Zumba, dance, etc.; exercise can help you reach your physical goals and keep you in good shape along with making the right eating choices. There are many positive benefits to exercising like having a better attitude and more self-confidence, which we already discussed that you will need as a successful model.

Another thing that you will need to invest in as a model is your skin. Clean your skin twice a day and exfoliate once a week so your natural self can always look its best. As a model if you struggle with skin problems like acne, it can cause you to have insecurities about how you look. Having a healthy skin regimen can reduce aging, control acne, and reduce pores and bumps.

I use to struggle with really dark circles underneath my eyes and that caused me to be insecure about the way that I looked. Once I started to change how I ate, drank

and took care of my skin; my dark circles disappeared and

my confidence went up. Now I love how my skin looks. I

cut back drastically on soda and began to drink a lot of

water which helps to also regulate my body weight. My

exercise has helped me to maintain my figure as a model

and, now I am satisfied in how I look and feel. I still have

goals but for the most part I am content.

Chapter 8
Look Like a Model

When people see you do they see a model or do you look contrary to what a model looks like? Do you just throw anything on or do you take the time out to be selective in what you wear?

If you are trying to go into modeling, it is important that you look like a model. If you are already a model, maintain your model look and upgrade if necessary. Dress where you are going in life. Practice what you are about to walk into. Dress like the world is your runway. Every time you step outside your door to go to your job, club, church, store, or any other destination, the first thing people see is how you look and dress.

Be selective in how you dress. You can't look like you got out of bed and you can't look like you don't invest in your style. Remember, how you look reveals how you see yourself and what you believe about yourself. We all have our days where we may not look our best, but you can't make it a habit. Even on those days find a way to make yourself look like a model. It can be something as simple as putting on some lip gloss or lipstick or adding accessories to your wardrobe to make it pop.

Every model has her personal swag and style, but one thing that will never change in the modeling world are high heels. As a model you should start wearing heels to different places. I'm not telling you to wear them every day, but you should wear them 2-3 times a week. Start making it a habit if you have not done so already. Wear heels that are comfortable and that you feel confident in. When you have to walk the runway, you will be better prepared because of your time wearing heels and getting your practice in.

Always keep your hair neat and styled as a model. You want to keep something on your face whether you just have lip gloss on or you have a full beat face. I know I don't wear makeup every day, but I do keep lip gloss on my lips at least. When people see you, they should say and think, "she looks like a model" or "she looks like someone out of a high print magazine!" Most importantly, it is easier for you to see yourself as a model when you dress the part.

Chapter 9
Network Defines Your
Model Net Worth

Your network defines your net worth as a model. Who you connect with and form a partnership with will determine the level of faith you have in yourself. It is important as a model to have people in your circle that support you and help you build your confidence. These supportive people can offer you opportunities that you wouldn't have otherwise discovered on your own, however, having the wrong network can detour you, and bring discouragement to you. It will cause you to doubt your path.

Having a strong network as a model opens doors for you to continue to grow your talent as well as your self-esteem. The more exposure you receive from the opportunities you take advantage of as a model, the stronger you will feel about your ability to model. Having a strong network is more than the number of people in it. The strength in your network comes from the quality of people that are connected to you. What counts is what they are adding to you in return for your service.

When you know that you have the right network, you are happy to use them as references to build your portfolio. It is a great feeling knowing that you have a supportive circle. When people ask you questions about your network, you will be more than ready to tell them about it rather than be ashamed and embarrassed about being connected to the wrong people.

My net worth came from surrounding myself with the right people. My runway coach, Tweety, connected me to Accentuate Boutique that I now model for. Other connections came from people who recommended me for shows and model groups online. Your network can come

from a variety of sources, so you should always use

wisdom and be open to how they appear in your life.

Remember, making smart decisions about your network

will strengthen your confidence and determine your value

as a model.

Acknowledgments

I would first like to thank God for giving me the talent to effectively communicate and inspire so many people through my writing. Next, I would like to thank Karen Ellen and the Listed Management team for encouraging me to write this book. I would like to thank everyone who supports me in my modeling and the people who have mentored me in my modeling. A special thanks to Jared White for the artwork in this book and KeAira Rogers for editing my book. I thank you, the reader, for supporting me by taking the time to read it and I hope that you find inspiration from it in your journey as a model.

About the Author

Xavier Gelsey is a fashion print and runway model who models for Accentuate Boutique in Jacksonville, Florida. She has been featured in the boutique's magazine as well as in the Local Star Newspaper and CW17. She has done local photoshoots as well as photoshoots in Jamaica and the Bahamas. You can find her on Facebook as @Xavier Gelsey and Instagram @Zayclatchet. Her motivation behind this book is to help and inspire girls and women to have confidence in themselves which is the ultimate foundation for modeling. Send your testimonies from the book to Xavier.gelsey@gmail.com.

www.ingramcontent.com/pod-product-compliance
Lightning Source LLC
Chambersburg PA
CBHW070520220526
45467CB00002B/767